Amici del Lago

BEST-LOVED ITALIAN RECIPES

Amici del Lago

JOSEPH SAFINA

For my wife, Amanda. Thank you for inspiring and supporting me for all these years.

For my sons Cole, Vince, and Luke. My hope is that you boys are inspired to continue the Safina tradition of cooking to bring friends and family together.

Cent'anni!

First published 2024

CONTENTS

Living on the Lake

The inspiration behind this book comes from Coeur D'Alene, Idaho—it is where we have a summer home and have spent the past decade making family memories for a lifetime. The topography reminded my wife and me of summer in Lake Cuomo, Italy. Being an eight-hour trip from Florida, it seemed so irrational for us to claim a second home there; ultimately, that home is exactly what we decided we couldn't live without. What's all the fuss about Idaho, you ask? No need to dig deeper—Idaho is all potato fields and muddy waters...nothing more to see here!

As time went on, we met truly great people. Our children made best friends; it was summer camp for kids and adults.

Our friendships grew, as did our dinner parties. The party was getting bigger every year, and our cottage was too small to handle the amazing group of friends that we are so blessed to have in our lives, so I decided to rent out an outdoor restaurant called the Orchard. This was the perfect venue. The kitchen faced the tables outdoors with a fireplace that took me back to my big dinners in Brooklyn, and an amazing setting that added an elegance that could not be duplicated anywhere else.

Our first year at the Orchard, there were 85 people. I shared the cooking with my great friend Kelly Chase, who has amazing cooking skills, along with Chef Kevin. Although I was confident, it was great to have support in the kitchen. The menu was epic. It started out with cheesesteak sandwiches, followed by my famous eggplant stack, spicy rigatoni, chicken cutlets Parmigiana, followed by hand-filled cannolis. The night was a great success...with the exception of me forgetting that I had sauce on the stove and then burning it. I had to start from scratch with two hours until dinner. Luckily, I managed to find just enough San Marzano tomatoes and basil to get it done (thanks, Jackie and Angela).

The next year Kelly and I faced enormous pressure to hit the repeat. We literally had people asking for us to do two dinner rotations! We finally folded under the pressure and did it again. This time we had well over 100 people. Except for our lobster stuffed with crabmeat in a lemon butter sauce starter, we stuck to the same menu. Kelly suggested doing a chicken piccata instead of the Parmigiana, and it came out epic. This time we had more help with Russ Courtnall and Chef Kevin's son, Shamus. The occasion was very special to me because we were all comfortable with one another, the wine was flowing in the kitchen, and we laughed until our faces hurt. The guests were as shocked as we were that we pulled it off in style, with flavors that were as vibrant as the beautiful setting of the Orchard.

Further motivation for the book is the many text messages I receive throughout the year from friends requesting recipes. My favorite message comes from my dear friend Shannon, who, every year, two days before Christmas, texts me asking for my Peter Lugar Filet Mignon Roast recipe. I simply cut and paste it from the previous year, but getting her text is my Christmas kickoff. On Christmas Eve she goes into a slight panic. I walk her through what to do, followed by her photo updates of the meal.

My Italian Roots

grew up in an Italian neighborhood in Bensonhurst, Brooklyn; it had a tough reputation to say the least. My mom was from Naples, and my dad, from Sicily. Although growing up in Brooklyn was complicated at times, it was a great place to be a kid. I enjoyed a childhood of playing stickball, dodging fire hydrants, and running around with friends until the sun went down, then playing cards and eating epic meals with chefs who passed their techniques and recipes down through each generation.

My grandparents on my mother's side lived in an old apartment building. Whenever I was hungry, I simply yelled up to my Grandma, who would open the window and ask, "Whatta you want?" I'd say, "Grandma, I'm hungry!" The smile on her face will remain in my memories forever. "Hold on, I make a sand-a-wich." Within five minutes she would lower a basket on a rope from her fifth-floor window with the best sandwiches. Sometimes it was leftover meatballs with fresh mozzarella and a few leaves of fresh basil off the plant she kept on her fire escape; other times it was mortadella, sausage and peppers, potato and eggs, peppers and eggs—whatever she sent down was always on fresh soft, hot Italian bread.

Sunday mornings, I would wake up to gravy, meatballs, and sausage cooking on the stove. The smell gave me such great comfort that the family was together. The family extended to cousins, aunts, uncles, friends, and whoever was in need that week. The neighborhood was very close. It was not uncommon for someone to be a little short on money and need to eat at a friend's house. This led to me getting a job at 12 years old at a local pizzeria. It wasn't long before I was making pizza, calzones, zeppoles, and many other Italian comfort foods.

I moved on, working at various restaurants and catering halls in Brooklyn, learning a little from everyone. At a fairly young age I was pursuing my dream

of becoming a professional race car driver. I had the opportunity to travel around Europe, working at various restaurants on the way to make ends meet, again picking up new techniques from France, Germany, Italy, and Canada. I was working in small family restaurants learning about different cultures, yet always with the common thread of a shared passion for food and cooking reminiscent of my childhood.

Many years later, my wife and I were traveling through Europe. After visiting Pompeii my wife posted a picture on Facebook and the next morning she got a message from my distant cousin who had spotted it. After a bit of back and forth with cousin Tino, we were invited to his home for Sunday dinner in a town outside of Naples called Brusciana. We decided it was definitely worth the trip, so we took the ferry from Capri to Naples and made the hour-long drive to Brusciana. The ride was long and windy, and as we neared the town, the landscape became more industrial. Not knowing what we might find, we made a final turn off the main street and pulled up to a metal gate behind a Fiat repair shop. As the gate opened, we were greeted by the sight of long tables, layed with mismatching checkered tablecloths, seating for 40 guests, and all of my relatives standing and clapping around them. They cooked a traditional Neapolitan Sunday dinner, and it was amazing. Although we had never met this long-lost family, we felt at home. We stayed for hours as food kept on coming. It was an amazing experience and a highlight of our trip, and although our Italian was rusty, we still managed to share stories and eat amazing food.

Cooking is the Italian language of love. Get creative. Change these recipes to make them your own, but most of all, cook with love and passion, not the stress of following a recipe. Pour a glass of wine and throw your measuring cups away. Just cook! I hope you enjoy *Amici del Lago* and it helps to build your own food memories.

I love to cook, but when I do, I don't measure, weigh, or follow recipes, so it was a challenge to put all this on paper. I hope you enjoy.

Joseph Safina

My Kitchen "Must Haves"

(all available on Amazon)

Utensils

16-inch frying pan

10-inch crepe pan

Immersion blender

Cupboard Supplies

Orzata (almond syrup)

Peter Luger steak sauce

Tutto Calabria peppers

Olio Verde extra-virgin olive oil

Gentile pasta

Stonewall Kitchen buttermilk pancake and waffle mix

San Marzano whole and crushed tomatoes

Garlic powder

Kosher salt

Caputo flour

Firelli Italian hot sauce

Italian lemon-flavored Brioschi (when you overeat)

What to Cook and When

Sometimes, there is only one dish that will suit the occasion!

Football Sunday
Chicken Wings and Roll-N-Roaster Sandwich
with Au Jus and Cheese Sauce or
Brooklyn Gourmet Cheesesteak

After a night of drinking
Hangover Breakfast Sandwich

For a romantic breakfast on a birthday or special occasion
Lemon Ricotta Pancakes. For breakfast in bed, go with Fig Toast.

Holidays
Filet Mignon Roast, Safina Spicy Rigatoni, and Watermelon Arugula Salad

Large parties
Eggplant Stack, Brooklyn Gourmet Cheesesteak,
and Chicken Cutlets Parmigiana

Romantic night at home
Linguine with Clams

Sunday tradition
Sunday Gravy

Gambling debt got out of hand
Lobster Francese

Bought a new watch without telling your wife, or bought a new bag without telling your husband
Linguine with Clams

Stayed on the golf course too long and she says she didn't cook
Chicken Francese

Crashed the new car your husband bought for you
Start the day with Fireball French Toast, followed by Broccoli Rabe and Sausage over Orecchiette for lunch and L'Entrecôte Steak with French Fries for dinner. He will forget about the car by the morning.

If you want a new car
Day one: Fig Toast for breakfast
Day two: Eggplant Stack for lunch
Day three: Filet Mignon Roast
for dinner (ask for the car)

EGGPLANT STACK

EGGPLANT CHIPS

BRAISED ARTICHOKE WITH MINT

POACHED PEARS WITH BURRATA
AND PROSCIUTTO

EGGPLANT ROLLATINI

SCUNGILLI

MOZZARELLA EN CARROZZA

CHICKEN WINGS

ITALIAN STUFFED PEPPERS

APPETIZERS

Eggplant Stack

SERVES 2

1 large eggplant, cut into ¼-inch slices

Pinch of kosher salt

2 cups vegetable oil

1 cup flour

1 cup seasoned breadcrumbs

16 ounces fresh mozzarella, cut into ¼-inch slices

1 large heirloom tomato, sliced

1 fresh basil leaf per stack

Pinch of freshly ground pepper to taste

Dash of extra-virgin olive oil

Dash of balsamic glaze

Handful of mixed greens

FOR THE EGG WASH

2 or 3 large eggs

Pinch of kosher salt

Pinch of freshly ground pepper

1 tablespoon Pecorino Romano

¼ cup finely chopped parsley

Garlic powder

METHOD

1. Lay the eggplant slices on a paper towel and generously salt both sides. Let sit for a half hour. This will pull the bitterness and the moisture out of the eggplant. (You will use 2 slices per stack.)

2. Prepare the egg wash: In a bowl mix the eggs with salt, pepper, Pecorino Romano, parsley, and garlic powder.

3. Heat the vegetable oil in a frying pan to about 300°F or use a deep fryer.

4. Set up two dishes: one with flour and one with breadcrumbs.

5. Gently dry each eggplant slice with a paper towel, dip both sides in flour, then in the egg wash, followed by the breadcrumbs, and drop into the hot oil. Cook until golden brown.

6. Place 1 fried eggplant slice on a serving dish. Add a mozzarella slice, a tomato slice, a full leaf of basil, salt, pepper, olive oil, and balsamic glaze. Place another eggplant slice on top and finish with the mixed greens, salt, pepper, olive oil, and balsamic glaze.

7. Repeat with the remaining slices.

Eggplant Chips

While vacationing in Spain my wife and I stumbled upon this delightful dish. *Berenjenas con miel* (aka crispy eggplant with honey) is a popular Spanish tapa with super crispy eggplant chips served with honey. Best of all, this dish requires just five ingredients and takes less than an hour for a delicious sweet and savory appetizer or side!

SERVES 2	METHOD
1 eggplant	1. Slice the eggplant thinly (this works best with a slicer). Traditionally, you cut the eggplant into long, thin slices, but you can also cut it into rounds.
Kosher salt	
1 cup milk	2. Salt both sides of the eggplant slices and place on a paper towel for 15 minutes, then soak in the milk for 30 minutes.
2 cups potato starch or cornstarch	
2 cups flour	3. Combine the potato starch (or cornstarch) and flour. Add the salt and pepper.
Freshly ground pepper to taste	
Vegetable oil	4. Cover both sides of the slices in the starch-flour mixture, pressing the slices into the mixture to make sure the mixture sticks to both sides.
Molasses for garnishing	
3 tablespoons honey	5. Heat up a frying pan with vegetable oil (enough to cover the eggplant) until it reaches 350°F, then cook the eggplant slices until golden brown. Place on a paper towel to absorb excess oil.
Dash of balsamic vinegar	
	6. Place the eggplant slices on a plate. Drip the molasses on top and generously salt.
	7. In a small bowl, mix the honey and balsamic vinegar to use as a side dipping sauce.

Braised Artichoke with Mint

1 28-ounce can whole San Marzano
tomatoes, drained

1½ cups dry white wine

Crushed red pepper flakes

2 teaspoons kosher salt

1 cup extra-virgin olive oil, divided

2 cups water

6 medium artichokes

2 lemons, halved

FOR THE PESTO

8–10 garlic cloves

1 cup (lightly packed) mint leaf

To Make the Pesto

Pulse the garlic in a food processor until finely chopped. Add the mint and pulse until coarsely chopped. With the motor running, stream in the remaining oil. Process until a coarse paste forms. Set aside.

To Make the Artichokes

1. Place the tomatoes in a large Dutch oven or other heavy pot and crush with your hands. Add the wine, red pepper flakes, salt, ½ cup olive oil, and water; set aside.

2. Remove several layers of dark-green outer leaves from each artichoke (keep going until you get to the tender light green leaves). Using a serrated knife, cut off the top 1 inch of each artichoke and trim the stem ends. Rub the cut ends with lemon halves to prevent browning.

3. Working with 1 artichoke at a time, use a paring knife or vegetable peeler to remove the tough outer green layer from the base and stem to reveal pale green underneath. Rub all over with lemon. Halve through the stem and rub the cut sides with more lemon. Use a spoon to scoop out the choke, then pull out the spiky inner leaves. Rub the insides with lemon. Rub the reserved pesto all over the artichoke halves and place in a single layer inside the Dutch oven or pot, submerging in the tomato mixture.

4. Bring to a simmer over medium-low heat and cook for 1 hour, turning the artichokes occasionally, until hearts are fork-tender. Transfer the artichokes to a platter and tent with foil to keep warm.

5. Increase the heat to medium, bring the sauce to a boil, and cook until slightly thickened, 10–15 minutes. Taste and season with more salt if needed. Spoon the sauce over the artichokes.

Poached Pears with Burrata and Prosciutto

SERVES 8

2 cups full-bodied red wine, such as a California cabernet or an Italian Barolo

2 cups water

1 cup sugar

1 cinnamon stick

6 cloves

3 thick slices of lemon

8 firm Comice or Bosc pears

½ pound prosciutto di Parma

8 small balls of burrata

5 fresh figs, cut in half (optional)

Pine nuts for garnishing

1. Combine the wine, water, sugar, cinnamon stick, cloves, and lemon slices in a saucepan. Bring to a boil and simmer, uncovered, until the mixture is reduced to approximately 4 cups liquid. Set aside until ready to use.

2. Preheat the oven to 350°F. Peel the pears but leave the stems on. Place the pears upright in a baking dish just large enough to hold them comfortably. Bring the wine mixture to a boil again and pour it over the pears (it will not cover them completely). Bake for 1 hour, basting every 15 minutes. The pears should darken to a rich mahogany color as they cook.

3. When the pears are done (still firm but easily pierced with a fork), remove them from the oven. The liquid in the baking dish should be syrupy. If it is not, transfer it to a saucepan and cook on the stove over a high heat until there are approximately 2 cups of syrup.

4. Place the pears in compote or similar dishes and cover with the syrup.

5. Place the pears on a plate with the prosciutto, burrata, and figs. Sprinkle the leftover syrup over the burrata and prosciutto and garnish with pine nuts.

Eggplant Rollatini

Eggplant rollatini is a dish that consists of thinly sliced eggplant that is traditionally dusted with flour and then "rolled" up with a ricotta and herb filling. It was created as a more affordable alternative to veal rollatini, a dish popular in Rome. Since first-generation Italian American immigrants couldn't afford veal, they replaced it with cheaper, more easily found eggplant.

SERVES 4

2 large eggplants, cut into ¼-inch slices

15 ounces ricotta

½ cup Parmigiano Reggiano, divided

1 egg

Pinch of kosher salt

Pinch of freshly ground pepper

2 garlic cloves, minced

½ cup fresh basil, torn

Marinara sauce

1 cup shredded mozzarella

METHOD

1. Salt the eggplant on both sides with a small pinch of coarse salt. Let it "sweat" the excess moisture out for 10 minutes, then pat dry with paper towels and wipe off the remaining salt.

2. Preheat the oven to 350°F. Lay the eggplant on a lightly greased pan and bake for 10 minutes. Remove and let cool.

3. In a small bowl, mix the ricotta, ¼ cup Parmigiano Reggiano, egg, salt, pepper, garlic, and basil. Then spoon 1–2 tablespoons of the ricotta filling onto the bottom of an eggplant slice. Roll it up and repeat.

4. In a baking dish, spoon half the marinara sauce onto the bottom and then place the eggplant rolls on top. Spoon the remaining sauce over the eggplant rolls, then top with the mozzarella and the remaining ¼ cup Parmigiano Reggiano. Cover the dish with foil and bake for 30 minutes, then remove the foil and bake for 10 more minutes, uncovered. Remove from the oven and enjoy!

Scungilli

Another 15-minute Italian classic using *scungilli* (conch).

SERVES 4	METHOD
¼ cup extra-virgin olive oil 4 garlic cloves 1 28-ounce can crushed San Marzano tomatoes 10 cherry tomatoes, cut in half ½ teaspoon Calabria peppers (Tutto) 1 29-ounce can scungilli (La Monica)	1. In a large frying pan add the olive oil and garlic. Once the garlic is golden brown (do not burn), add the crushed tomatoes and mix constantly. 2. Add the cherry tomatoes and Calabria peppers and cook for about 5 minutes. 3. Strain the can of scungilli (reserving some of the water) and add to the sauce. Stir for about 5 minutes at low heat. Taste the sauce and add salt as needed. 4. Serve over garlic bread (see page 109).

Mozzarella en Carrozza

A fried mozzarella sandwich. This Neapolitan
comfort food can be made in five minutes.

SERVES 4	METHOD
4 slices of mortadella	1. Crisp the mortadella in a frying pan. Dry the mozzarella slices with a paper towel. Cut the crust off the bread slices.
4 to 8 slices of mozzarella	
8 slices of white bread	2. Mix the eggs with the salt, pepper, and Pecorino Romano.
4 eggs	
Pinch of kosher salt to taste	3. Place a mortadella slice, sun-dried tomatoes or peppers, a full basil leaf, 1 or 2 mozzarella slices, and pepper on a slice of bread and top with a slice of bread. Repeat to make 4 sandwiches. Dip the sandwiches in the flour, followed by the egg bath, then cover completely in the breadcrumbs.
Pinch of freshly ground pepper to taste	
¼ cup Pecorino Romano, plus more for garnishing	
5 sun-dried tomatoes or peppers	
4 fresh basil leaves	4. Fry in olive oil over medium heat until golden brown on both sides. Cut in half and serve over marinara sauce, garnished with a generous amount of Pecorino Reggiano.
½ cup flour	
Panko breadcrumbs	
Extra-virgin olive oil	
Marinara sauce	

Chicken Wings

SERVES 4

¼ cup extra-virgin olive oil

½ cup finely chopped whole garlic cloves

3 cups chicken bone broth

1 cup sweet chili sauce

1 tablespoon hoisin sauce

¼ teaspoon chopped Calabria peppers (Tutto)

2 tablespoons unsalted butter

Flour

¼ cup vegetable oil

30 chicken wings

1 tablespoon sesame seeds

2 scallions, chopped

1. Heat the olive oil in a saucepan and cook the garlic until golden brown. Add the bone broth, chili sauce, and hoisin sauce, bring to a boil, drop to a low temperature, and let simmer until reduced by half. Once reduced, add the Calabria peppers. Dredge the butter in flour and whisk into the sauce until thick.

2. Heat the vegetable oil to 350°F and fry the wings. Look for a crispy brown color and an internal temperature of 165°F. Toss in the sauce and serve. Finish with sesame seeds and scallions.

Italian Stuffed Peppers

SERVES 6

6 bell peppers (any color), cut in half, seeds removed

2 medium sausages

½ pound ground beef

1½ pounds ground veal

2 ounces Pecorino Romano

⅓ cup minced garlic cloves

Fresh basil, chopped

2 cups cooked rice

Pinch of kosher salt

Pinch of freshly ground pepper

Dried chili flakes to taste

8 ounces fresh mozzarella, grated

4 cups marinara sauce

METHOD

1. Preheat the oven to 450°F.

2. Place the peppers on a baking sheet and bake until the peppers begin to roast, about 20 minutes. I like to put them over an open flame on the stove to get a char prior to going into the oven.

3. Remove the sausage meat from the casings and place in a bowl with the ground beef and ground veal.

4. Mix in the Pecorino Romano, garlic, basil, cooked rice, salt, pepper, and dried chili flakes.

5. Stuff the roasted peppers with the mixture and top off with the mozzarella and marinara sauce. I like to put a bit of the sauce on before and once again after the mozzarella.

6. Bake for about 10 minutes until the mozzarella is fully melted. Top with the basil and Pecorino Romano.

FILET MIGNON ROAST

SAUSAGE AND PEPPERS

CHICKEN FRANCESE

L'ENTRECÔTE STEAK WITH FRENCH FRIES

SALTIMBOCCA ALLA ROMANA

CHICKEN CUTLETS PARMIGIANA

CHICKEN THREE WAYS

LOBSTER FRANCESE

CHICKEN MARSALA

BRAISED SHORT RIBS

LAMB SCOTTADITO

AMANDA'S CHICKEN

MAPLE MISO GLAZED SALMON

ENTRÉES

Filet Mignon Roast

This is a Christmas favorite. My wife's best friend Shannon has called me every year for the past seven years to ask me for the recipe. I have resorted to cutting and pasting the recipe from our text exchanges. Shannon's calls have become the true start of the Christmas feast as she gets me into cook mode. She was part of the motivation to write this book. It is a great compliment that she built her tradition around one of my original recipes. Shannon will be one of the first to receive this book, on second thought. I love hearing from her, so maybe I will rip this page out.

The steak sauce is from the famous Peter Luger Steak House of Brooklyn. "Carl Luger's Café, Billiards and Bowling Alley" opened in 1887 and quickly became a neighborhood favorite in predominantly German Williamsburg. Peter Luger owned the establishment in the 1920s, and it became a world-class steak house.

SERVES 5

5 pounds or more filet mignon roast

1 tablespoon kosher salt

½ tablespoon freshly ground pepper

1 cup clarified butter

3 bottles Peter Luger steak sauce

½ cup extra-virgin olive oil

5 garlic cloves

METHOD

1. Start with a high-quality filet mignon roast with the fat trimmed and tied off if necessary. Place the roast in a bowl with the salt, pepper, butter, and steak sauce. Let the roast sit for a few hours to ensure that the meat is at room temperature.

2. Line your stove with aluminum foil because this makes a huge mess. Preheat the oven to 400°F.

3. In a large frying pan (the roast can be split in two if you do not have a pan large enough) over high heat, heat the olive oil, then fry the garlic until golden brown. Remove the garlic and set aside.

4. Place the roast in the hot oil (set aside the clarified butter mixture) and pour a ½ bottle of Peter Luger steak sauce on top. Be sure to brown all sides until slightly crispy. The sugar in the steak sauce will caramelize, building a delicious outer layer.

5. Once the roast is browned on all sides, place it in a baking pan. Pour the clarified butter mixture on top of the roast and salt the roast. Bake until medium-rare at the center (about 10 minutes per pound but check the temperature after 5 minutes per pound), adding the other half of the Peter Luger steak sauce about halfway through.

6. Let the meat sit for about 10 minutes, then cut into ½-inch slices and place on a serving dish. Pour a bit of the steak sauce on top and serve.

Sausage and Peppers

Brooklyn was known for its feasts. The big feast was Santa Rosalia on 18th Avenue, the highlight of the neighborhood with food trucks, rides, and relatives visiting from all over New York. It was the Brooklyn version of the famed San Generio Feast in Little Italy. It was also an opportunity to make money, so I would work the sausage and pepper stand for Crazy Vinny. Crazy Vinny hated change, but I suggested we grill the bread with a garlic spread. We tried it and everyone loved it.

Our specialty was zeppoles and sausage and peppers. I approached Vinny with an idea of a dipping sauce for the zeppoles made with mascarpone, brown sugar, cinnamon, and fresh mint. Once again everyone loved it. Our line was always the longest.

Once I was making a big pile of sausage and peppers when I made what I thought was a big mistake. Instead of butter I slammed a ladleful of mascarpone cheese on the sausage and peppers. I panicked for a second, then tried to cover it up with a slab of butter, at which point I had Crazy Vinny threatening to stab me in the leg. While he was yelling in a dialect of Italian I could barely understand (but I knew he was pissed), I decided to hit it with a bit of heavy cream and make a sandwich to see what it would taste like. I cut the sandwich in half, now out of reach of Crazy Vinny, and we both took a bite. The creamy, sweet, savory sauce penetrating the hot toasted garlic bread was messy but delicious. We served the batch and asked everyone what they thought, and we got rave reviews.

Crazy Vinny went on to add butter and mascarpone to his sausage and pepper sandwiches and was as successful as a broken-down sausage and pepper trailer could be. Manga!

SERVES 4

½ cup extra-virgin olive oil

2 garlic cloves

2 yellow peppers, sliced

2 red peppers, sliced

1 large onion, sliced

Kosher salt to taste

Freshly ground pepper to taste

1 tablespoon mascarpone

1 cup heavy cream

2 hot Italian sausage links, cut into
½-inch rounds

2 sweet Italian sausage links, cut
into ½-inch rounds

Ciabatta bread

2 tablespoons unsalted butter

FOR THE GARLIC SPREAD

3 garlic cloves

1 stick unsalted butter

Handful of fresh chopped parsley

Pinch of kosher salt

Pinch of freshly ground pepper

METHOD

1. Preheat the oven to 350°F. Prepare the garlic spread by combining all the garlic spread ingredients.

2. Heat up the olive oil in a large frying pan to about 300°F and cook the garlic until golden brown. Remove and discard the garlic.

3. Add the peppers and onions to the pan and reduce the heat. Generously salt and pepper the mixture, turning constantly. Once the peppers are softened a bit, add the mascarpone and heavy cream. Keep turning the mixture until the mascarpone is fully dissolved. Remove the mixture from the frying pan and place in a bowl.

4. Heat a small amount of olive oil in a frying pan and drop in the sausage rounds.

5. Cut open a loaf of ciabatta bread, remove the filling, and brush on the garlic spread. Bake until the bread is crispy, about 2–3 minutes.

6. Once the sausage is about three-quarters of the way cooked, place the peppers and onion mixture into the frying pan and lower the heat for about 5 minutes. Stir in the butter.

7. Remove the bread from the oven and generously add the sausage and pepper mixture to the bread. With a spoon, drizzle the liquid from the frying pan onto the top. Cut and serve.

Chicken Francese

SERVES 4

2 pounds chicken cutlets

3 eggs

Kosher salt to taste

Freshly ground pepper to taste

¼ cup Pecorino Romano

½ cup finely chopped, fresh parsley

¾ cup extra-virgin olive oil

1 stick plus 1 tablespoon
unsalted butter, divided

3 garlic cloves

2 cups flour

½ cup white wine

2 cups chicken stock

Juice from 2 lemons

Lemon zest from ½ lemon

1. Pound the cutlets thin. Crack the eggs into a large bowl. Add the salt, pepper, Pecorino Romano, and parsley and beat.

2. In a large frying pan over low to medium heat, heat up the olive oil and 1 tablespoon butter. Add the garlic and cook until golden brown. Remove and discard the garlic.

3. Place the flour in a dish and fully cover the chicken cutlets with flour, then the egg bath. Place the cutlets in the hot oil. Cook until lightly browned on one side, about 3 minutes, and turn. (Lower the heat if the oil begins to get too hot.) Cook the other side for about 3 minutes. Remove the chicken and place on a paper towel to rest.

4. Discard the oil and deglaze the pan over low heat by dipping the stick of butter in the flour and rubbing the stick around the pan. Dip the stick back into the flour to thicken the mixture as desired. Once the butter is fully melted, add the white wine and continue to deglaze the pan with a wooden spoon for about 30 seconds. Add the chicken stock, salt, and pepper and let the sauce thicken.

5. Add the chicken back into the pan. Add the lemon juice and lemon zest into the sauce, as well as a generous amount of parsley. Taste the sauce and adjust the seasoning as desired. Let the chicken cook in the sauce for about 5 minutes.

L'Entrecôte Steak with French Fries

One of the best steaks I've ever had in my life was at a L'Entrecôte restaurant in Paris, France. The restaurant sold just grilled steaks slathered with a creamy yellow butter-based sauce and served with matchstick fries. Since then, I have tried to duplicate the sauce for years, and I finally figured it out. The sauce is magic.

SERVES 4

Ribeye or Delmonico steak
Kosher salt
Freshly ground pepper

FOR THE SAUCE
3 sticks unsalted butter
3 shallots, chopped
3 sage leaves
¼ cup chopped parsley
Pinch of tarragon
3 fresh basil leaves
½ teaspoon grated nutmeg
1 tablespoon capers
5 anchovy fillets in olive oil
1 egg yolk
1 tablespoon Worcestershire sauce
1 tablespoon Dijon mustard

METHOD

1. Generously salt and pepper both sides of the steak. I like to barbecue the steaks, but you can cook them in a skillet. Cook steaks until they are rare to medium. Do not overcook.

2. Slice the steaks and place on a plate with the french fries and drench it with the sauce.

To Make the Sauce

1. Melt 1 stick of the butter over low heat with the shallots and sage leaves. Let simmer, but don't let the shallots get brown. Add all the remaining ingredients except the egg yolk, Worcestershire sauce, and Dijon mustard. Add the remaining 2 sticks of butter and let everything melt slowly together. Blend with a hand mixer or blender. Allow to cool slightly.

2. Mix the egg yolk, Worcestershire sauce, and Dijon mustard together in a bowl. Whisk vigorously while adding a little bit of the butter mixture at a time to create a smooth "mayonnaise."

3. Heat two-thirds of this "mayonnaise" in a saucepan (leave the rest in the bowl) until the sauce cracks. Reduce the heat to low for a few minutes. Let the sauce cool down and whisk with the "mayonnaise" again so that you get a semi-crispy sauce that covers the meat even better. This is the traditional French way of making this sauce. Now the sauce is ready to be enjoyed on the grilled steak.

FOR THE FRIES

4 large potatoes

1 cup potato starch

2 cups extra-virgin olive oil

Kosher salt to taste

Freshly ground pepper to taste

1 tablespoon dry parsley

To Make the French Fries

Cut the potatoes into thin strips and cover in the potato starch. Heat up the olive oil to 350°F and fry until golden brown. Place in a bowl and toss in the salt, pepper, and dry parsley. If you want to cheat, you can buy frozen french fries at the supermarket or hit the McDonald's drive-through (not kidding, the french fries are perfect for this dish).

Saltimbocca alla Romana

Saltimbocca consists of veal that has been wrapped with prosciutto and sage and then marinated in wine, oil, or salt water. The original version of this dish is *Saltimbocca alla Romana* ("Roman style"), which consists of veal, prosciutto, and sage, rolled up and cooked in dry white wine and butter. Marsala wine is sometimes used. Also, sometimes the veal and prosciutto are not rolled up but left flat. An American variation replaces the veal with chicken or pork.

SERVES 4	METHOD
8 slices of prosciutto	1. Place 1 slice of prosciutto on each veal scaloppine and pound in lightly with a meat pounder.
8 veal scaloppine, thinly sliced and pounded	
2 tablespoons extra-virgin olive oil	2. Heat the olive oil in a large sauté pan over medium-high heat. Dredge both sides of the scaloppine in flour to coat, shaking off any excess. Place them prosciutto side down in the pan and cook, turning once, until lightly browned on both sides. Transfer to a warm plate.
½ cup flour	
2 tablespoons unsalted butter	
8 sage leaves	
½ cup dry white wine	3. Drain the oil from the pan, place back over the heat, and add the butter. When the butter is melted, add the sage and sauté for 1 minute.
¼ cup chicken broth	
Kosher salt to taste	
Freshly ground pepper to taste	4. Add the white wine and scrape up any bits from the bottom of the pan, then add the chicken broth and salt and pepper.
	5. Place the scaloppine back in the pan, prosciutto side up, and cook until the sauce is reduced by half and the scaloppine are heated through.
	6. Transfer the veal to serving plates, 2 scaloppine per person, spoon sauce over the top, and serve.

Chicken Cutlets Parmigiana

My chicken Parm is a bit different. Most put the chicken cutlets in the oven to melt the cheese, which sometimes causes the chicken to overcook. It also separates the flavor profile. Try it this way and compare. Ask your butcher to pound your chicken cutlets thin. Alternatively, you can cover the cutlets with wax paper and pound them with a meat mallet.

SERVES 4

FOR THE EGG WASH

3 large eggs

Kosher salt

Freshly ground pepper

1 tablespoon finely grated Pecorino Romano

¼ cup chopped fresh parsley

Pinch of garlic powder

FOR THE BREADCRUMB MIXTURE

2 cups Italian seasoned breadcrumbs

¼ cup finely chopped fresh parsley

¼ cup Parmigiano Reggiano

FOR THE CHICKEN CUTLETS

4 6-ounce chicken cutlets, pounded thin

¼ teaspoon kosher salt

¼ teaspoon freshly ground pepper

¼ teaspoon garlic powder

1 cup flour

2 cups extra-virgin olive oil

2 garlic cloves, crushed, divided

Fresh mozzarella, cut into ¼-inch slices

METHOD

1. Prepare the egg wash and the breadcrumb mixture.

2. Season the chicken cutlets on both sides with salt, pepper, and garlic powder. Dredge the cutlets in the flour. Dip the cutlets in the egg mixture, then in the breadcrumbs, making sure both sides are covered.

3. In a large frying pan over medium heat, heat the olive oil. Add 1 garlic clove and cook until golden brown. Remove and discard the garlic.

4. Add the chicken cutlets and cook until golden brown on both sides. Remove from the oil and place on a paper towel.

5. Reconstitute the mozzarella by placing it in warm water for 20–30 minutes. Not a critical step but a nice touch.

FOR THE SAUCE

¼ cup extra-virgin olive oil

2 garlic cloves, crushed

1 28-ounce can crushed
San Marzano tomatoes

15 cherry tomatoes, cut in half

Kosher salt to taste

Freshly ground pepper to taste

¼ teaspoon granulated garlic

Fresh chopped basil for garnishing

1 tablespoon grated
Parmigiano Reggiano

6. Heat up the olive oil in a frying pan over medium heat. Add the remaining garlic and cook until golden brown. Add the crushed tomatoes and lower the heat. Add the cherry tomatoes, salt, pepper, garlic, basil, and Parmigiano Reggiano. Cook over medium heat for 15 minutes, followed by high heat for 15 minutes, stirring consistently.

7. Plate the cutlets, add a slice of mozzarella on top, then the sauce. Top with Parmigiano Reggiano and fresh basil. The sauce will melt the mozzarella and deliver a unique flavor profile.

Chicken Three Ways

SERVES 4

Chicken Cutlets Parmigiana
(see page 46)

Broccoli rabe (see page 106)

5 slices of provolone

Arugula

FOR THE SALAD DRESSING

2 tablespoons champagne or white
wine vinegar

Pinch of kosher salt

Pinch of freshly ground pepper

6 tablespoons extra-virgin olive oil

Juice of 2 lemons

METHOD

1. Prepare the cutlets from the Chicken Cutlets Parmigiana recipe (up to step 4) and the broccoli rabe.

2. Prepare the salad dressing and toss with the arugula.

3. Top one-third of the chicken cutlets with the mozzarella slices and sauce (see Chicken Cutlets Parmigiana recipe).

4. Top one-third of the chicken cutlets with the broccoli rabe and provolone slices.

5. Top the final one-third of the chicken cutlets with the dressed arugula and some freshly grated Pecorino Romano.

6. Serve on three separate platters. I usually cut the finished cutlets in half so everyone can taste each of the three recipes.

Lobster Francese

SERVES 1

FOR THE EGG WASH

2 eggs

Pinch of kosher salt

Pinch of freshly ground pepper

⅛ cup Parmigiano Reggiano

FOR THE LOBSTER

1 large lobster tail, deshelled
(keep the shell)

Kosher salt to taste

Freshly ground pepper to taste

Granulated garlic to taste

1 cup flour

Vegetable oil

3 garlic cloves

4 ounces unsalted butter

1 ounce white wine

2 ounces chicken stock

Juice of 3 large lemons

Parsley

1 can jumbo lump crabmeat

METHOD

1. Make the egg wash by blending all the ingredients together.

2. Season the lobster tail with the salt, pepper, and granulated garlic. Coat the lobster tail in the flour, then dip in the egg wash.

3. Fill the frying pan about 30% with the vegetable oil, heat up over medium heat, and add the garlic cloves. Once the garlic is golden brown, remove and discard.

4. Drop the lobster in the oil until it is golden brown on both sides. Remove the lobster and discard the oil.

5. Put the pan back on the heat and add the white wine and chicken stock. Dip the butter in the flour and whisk the mixture in until slightly thick. Add the lemon juice and parsley.

6. Take the lobster shell and stuff it with the crabmeat. Place on a dish with the lobster tail and pour the sauce on everything.

Chicken Marsala

SERVES 4

4 chicken cutlets, pounded thin

Kosher salt to taste

Freshly ground pepper to taste

¼ cup extra-virgin olive oil

1 cup flour

8 ounces button mushrooms

½ cup Marsala wine

½ cup chicken stock

2 tablespoons unsalted butter

¼ cup chopped fresh parsley

4 slices of fontina

METHOD

1. Pound the chicken with the flat side of a meat mallet. Salt and pepper both sides of the chicken.

2. In a medium saucepan, heat the olive oil over medium-high heat. Spread the flour onto a plate and coat the chicken breasts, making sure to shake off any excess flour.

3. When the oil is hot, sauté the chicken until golden brown (turning once), about 5 minutes on each side. Set aside.

4. Drain the olive oil out of the pan and sauté the mushrooms. Once the mushrooms have softened, add the Marsala wine and deglaze the pan. Add the chicken stock and simmer for a minute, then stir in the butter and add the chicken. Salt and pepper to taste and cook until the sauce thickens.

5. Put the chicken on a plate and spoon some of the remaining sauce mixture over top. Garnish with fresh parsley and fontina.

Braised Short Ribs

SERVES 4

5 pounds bone-in beef short ribs, cut crosswise into 2-inch pieces

Kosher salt to taste

Freshly ground pepper to taste

3 tablespoons vegetable oil

3 medium yellow onions, chopped

3 medium carrots, peeled and chopped

2 celery stalks, chopped

3 tablespoons flour

1 tablespoon tomato paste

1 750-ml bottle dry red wine (preferably Cabernet Sauvignon)

10 sprigs flat-leaf parsley

8 sprigs fresh thyme

4 sprigs fresh oregano

2 sprigs fresh rosemary

2 fresh or dried bay leaves

1 head of garlic, halved crosswise

4 cups low-sodium beef stock

1. Preheat the oven to 350°F. Season the short ribs with salt and pepper. Heat the vegetable oil in a large Dutch oven over medium-high heat. Working in two batches, brown the short ribs on all sides, about 8 minutes per batch. Transfer the short ribs to a plate. Pour off all but 3 tablespoons drippings from the pot.

2. Add the onions, carrots, and celery to the pot and cook over medium-high heat, stirring often, until the onions are golden brown, about 5 minutes. Add the flour and tomato paste. Cook, stirring constantly, until well combined and deep red, 2–3 minutes. Stir in the wine, then add the short ribs with any accumulated juices. Bring to a boil, then lower the heat to medium and simmer until the wine is reduced by half, about 25 minutes. Add all herbs to the pot along with the garlic. Stir in the stock. Bring to a boil, cover, and transfer to the oven.

3. Cook until the short ribs are tender, 2–2½ hours. Transfer the short ribs to a platter. Strain the sauce from the pot into a measuring cup. Spoon the fat from the surface of the sauce and discard. Season the sauce with salt and pepper.

Lamb Scottadito

Lamb scottadito translates into "burnt fingers" in Italian.
This dish is traditionally served in a hot skillet on a thick
cutting board. Everyone would reach in and grab a lamb
chop out of the hot skillet, hence the name.

SERVES 4	METHOD
8 lamb chops Extra-virgin olive oil 4 garlic cloves, smashed Fresh rosemary, chopped ½ teaspoon crushed Calabria peppers (Tutto) Juice of 4 lemons Pinch of garlic powder Pinch of kosher salt Pinch of freshly ground pepper ¼ cup high-temp olive oil ½ cup clarified butter Fresh basil for garnishing	1. Marinate overnight the lamb chops in enough olive oil to cover all the chops and the garlic, rosemary, Calabria peppers, lemon juice, garlic powder, salt, and pepper. 2. Heat up a skillet over high heat. Once hot, add the high-temp olive oil and clarified butter, then put the lamb chops in and pour the marinade on top. Cook, flipping once, until the meat is rare, about 1 minute per side. I recommend displaying on a serving platter so that you do not burn your fingers. Finish with extra-virgin olive oil and basil.

Amanda's Chicken

SERVES 4

2 medium onions

2 pounds carrots

1 pound celery

Olive oil

Kosher salt

Freshly ground pepper

1 4-pound whole chicken

2 lemons

1. Preheat the oven to 400°F. Chop the onions, carrots, and celery and put into a large roasting pan or glass baking dish. Generously season with olive oil, salt, and pepper. Mix until the vegetables are fully covered.

2. Place the vegetables in a greased dish and place in the oven for about 45 minutes, turning every 20 minutes.

3. Rinse the chicken under warm water. Squeeze the lemons inside the chicken and put inside the chicken. Drizzle olive oil and generously salt and pepper the top of the chicken and place on top of the cooked vegetables.

4. Cook the chicken and vegetables for about an hour (15–20 minutes per pound) until the chicken reaches about 165°F.

5. Remove from the oven and let sit for 10 minutes before serving.

Maple Miso Glazed Salmon

SERVES 4

3 tablespoons pure maple syrup

3 tablespoons reduced-sodium soy sauce

1 tablespoon sriracha hot sauce

1 clove garlic, smashed

4 6-ounce wild salmon fillets, skinless

METHOD

1. Combine the maple syrup, soy sauce, sriracha, and garlic in a small bowl, pour into a gallon-sized resealable bag, and add the salmon. Marinate for 30–60 minutes.

2. Preheat the oven to 400°F. Lightly grease a baking sheet with nonstick spray. Remove the fish from the marinade and pat dry with paper towels. Pour the marinade in a small saucepan.

3. Place the fish on the baking sheet and cook for 11–14 minutes. Meanwhile, bring the marinade to a simmer over medium heat and reduce until it thickens into a glaze. Spoon over the fish just before eating.

LINGUINE ALLE VONGOLE (LINGUINE WITH CLAMS)

MEATBALLS

SAFINA SPICY RIGATONI

MANICOTTI CREPES

PASTA ALLA NORMA

SUNDAY GRAVY

FAST SAUCE

MINT PESTO

BROCCOLI RABE AND SAUSAGE OVER ORECCHIETTE

SPAGHETTI AGLIO E OLIO

CACIO E PEPE

BUCATINI ALL'AMATRICIANA

LEMON PASTA WITH
SESAME SEEDS AND PECORINO ROMANO

Linguine alle Vongole
(Linguine with Clams)

SERVES 4

¼ cup extra-virgin olive oil, plus extra for topping

8 garlic cloves, smashed

Pinch of red pepper flakes or ⅛ teaspoon Calabria peppers (Tutto)

24 littleneck clams

1 cup white wine

Bunch of Italian parsley, roughly chopped

Kosher salt to taste

1 pound linguine

Lemon zest (optional)

METHOD

1. Heat the olive oil in a large saucepan over medium heat and allow the garlic to brown. Add a pinch of red pepper flakes or the Calabria peppers and mix in. Add the clams with the white wine and parsley and allow the clams to steam open. Remove the clams and set aside. Taste the sauce and add salt and more red pepper to taste.

2. Cook the linguine until it's half cooked, stirring occasionally, reserving about 1 cup of the pasta water. Add the linguine to the frying pan and gradually add some pasta water. When it is cooking at high heat, add your clams and finish with some extra-virgin olive oil. I sometimes finish with a bit of lemon zest as well.

Meatballs

MAKES 30 MEATBALLS

5 slices of Wonder bread or any soft white bread

1 cup milk

1 pound veal, room temperature

1 pound beef, room temperature

1 pound pork, room temperature

2 large eggs

¼ teaspoon crushed peppercorns

Kosher salt

Granulated garlic powder

2 cups finely chopped fresh parsley

2 cups Parmigiano Reggiano

1 cup Italian seasoned breadcrumbs

2 cups vegetable oil

METHOD

1. Soak the bread in milk until it's soft, then strain to get the excess milk out. Press a bit without pushing the bread through the strainer.

2. Put all the remaining ingredients in a bowl except for the vegetable oil and mix thoroughly with your hands.

3. In a deep frying pan over medium heat, add the vegetable oil. Make a mini meatball to test for flavor, adjusting the seasoning if necessary.

4. Start rolling your meatballs. Fry the meatballs for about 3 minutes per side depending on the size of the meatballs.

Safina Spicy Rigatoni

This dish was inspired by the great Mario Carbone of Carbone's Restaurant. One of my favorite dishes at Carbone's is the famous spicy rigatoni. I spent a lot of time modifying the recipe to make it different yet capturing the texture of this great dish.

SERVES 4

1 large onion, thinly sliced

4 sticks unsalted butter

Pinch of kosher salt

Pinch of flour

½ cup extra-virgin olive oil

1 28-ounce can crushed San Marzano tomatoes

1 teaspoon Calabria peppers (Tutto), more if needed

Pinch of freshly ground pepper

½ cup heavy cream

1 pound rigatoni

1 cup Parmigiano Romano

Fresh basil, hand-torn, for garnishing

METHOD

1. Place the onions in a medium-size pot with the butter over low heat. Add the salt and cook until the onions are translucent. Be sure not to burn the butter; you can shut the heat off from time to time if you need to lower the temperature. Add a few pinches of flour to thicken it up and whisk it in. Set the sauce aside.

2. In a large frying pan over medium heat, add the olive oil and tomatoes, Calabria peppers, salt, and pepper. After about 15 minutes, taste and adjust the salt and Calabria peppers as desired. I generally like more heat, so I usually add another spoonful. Add the heavy cream and half the onion mixture. Taste and adjust once again and add more of the onions and heavy cream as desired. It should have a bright pink color.

3. Cook the rigatoni until it's half cooked. Remove 1 cup of the pasta water and set aside. Drop the pasta in the frying pan and let it cook out. Thin the sauce as needed with the pasta water and add the Parmigiano Romano, continuing to stir. Taste the pasta, adjust your salt and Calabria peppers as needed, and serve, garnished with the basil.

Manicotti Crepes

Manicotti literally means "big sleeves." The crepes are the key to this elegant dish. As my grandmother would say, "Fry the crepe and pick it up. If you can't see through it, it's too thick."

SERVES 4	METHOD

FOR THE CREPES

6 large eggs

3 cups cold water

3 tablespoons corn oil

½ teaspoon kosher salt

3 cups flour

½ teaspoon vegetable oil

FOR THE FILLING

2 large eggs

1 teaspoon kosher salt

2 pounds ricotta

2 cups shredded mozzarella (about 10 ounces)

1 cup grated Parmigiano Reggiano (about 2 ounces)

1 tablespoon minced fresh flat-leaf parsley

Pinch of pepper

Pinch of nutmeg

FOR THE ASSEMBLED DISH

4 cups marinara sauce

1 cup grated Pecorino Romano, divided

To Make the Crepes

1. Mix all the ingredients and place the batter in the refrigerator for 30 minutes.

2. Remove the batter from the fridge and whisk it briefly. Heat the vegetable oil in an 8-inch nonstick pan over medium heat. Add about 3 tablespoons of batter, lifting and swirling the pan to spread a thin, even layer of batter on the bottom of the pan. Cook until the batter starts to appear dry, about 30 seconds, then carefully flip the crepe over and continue cooking for another 30 seconds. Transfer to a wire rack to cool. Repeat with the remaining crepe batter, adding oil every few crepes and adjusting heat as necessary.

To Make the Filling

In a large bowl, combine all the ingredients. Cover and refrigerate until ready to assemble the manicotti.

To Assemble the Dish

1. Preheat the oven to 375°F and lightly brush two 9-by-13-inch baking dishes with oil.

2. Spread 3–4 tablespoons of filling down the center of 1 crepe. Roll it up and place it, seam-side down, in one of the baking dishes. Repeat with the remaining crepes and filling.

3. Divide the marinara sauce between two baking dishes, spreading it evenly over the manicotti, then bake for 30 minutes. Sprinkle each baking dish with about ½ cup Pecorino Romano and continue baking until the sauce is bubbling and the cheese is just starting to brown, about 10 minutes more.

Pasta alla Norma

Formally known as *pasta con le melanzane*, which
translates to "pasta with eggplant." This is a traditional
Sicilian dish that I love on a cold winter day.

SERVES 4	METHOD
1 28-ounce can whole peeled San Marzano tomatoes	1. Place the tomatoes with juices into a medium bowl and crush the tomatoes with your hands. Set aside.
⅓ cup plus 2 tablespoons extra-virgin olive oil, divided	2. Heat ⅓ cup olive oil in a large Dutch oven or other heavy pot over medium-high heat. Add the eggplant and sprinkle with 1 teaspoon salt. Cook, stirring occasionally, until the eggplant is softened and golden brown, 6–8 minutes. Transfer to a bowl.
1 pound eggplant, cut into ½-inch pieces	
2 teaspoons kosher salt, divided	
3 garlic cloves, thinly sliced	3. Heat 2 tablespoons olive oil in the same pot over medium-high heat. Cook the garlic and crushed red pepper flakes, stirring constantly, until golden brown. Add the tomato paste and cook, stirring, until darkened in color, about 2 minutes. Add the oregano, 1 teaspoon salt, and tomatoes. Bring to a boil and cook, stirring occasionally, until the sauce is slightly thickened, about 5 minutes. Return the eggplant to the pot and cook, stirring occasionally, until the eggplant is completely tender.
½ teaspoon crushed red pepper flakes	
1 6-ounce can tomato paste	
2 tablespoons coarsely chopped oregano	
1 pound tubular pasta (such as calamarata or rigatoni)	
Pecorino Romano for topping	4. Cook the pasta, stirring occasionally, until al dente, reserving 1 cup pasta water.
4 ounces ricotta salata, shaved, for topping	5. Add the pasta and ½ cup pasta cooking liquid to the sauce. Cook, stirring often and adding more pasta cooking liquid if needed, until the sauce is thickened and coats the pasta, about 2 minutes.
Fresh basil, hand-torn, for garnishing	
Freshly ground pepper to taste	6. Divide the pasta among shallow bowls. Top with Pecorino Romano, ricotta salata, and basil. Season with freshly ground pepper.

Sunday Gravy

Growing up in Brooklyn we did not wake up on Sunday morning to the smell of coffee, bacon, and pancakes but instead to the smell of Sunday gravy. The entire apartment smelled like tomatoes and garlic. I remember tearing off a big piece of fresh, hot Italian bread that my grandmother bought at the bakery that morning, dipping it in the gravy, then adding a thick piece of fresh mozzarella that my grandfather made from scratch every Sunday, and that was the Italian breakfast of champions. Whenever I cook my gravy, it takes me back to that two-bedroom apartment across from the train station with that Sunday smell. Nothing is more comforting.

The debate on whether it's sauce or gravy will live on as an Italian territorial battle. Being Sicilian, it's gravy. You call it what you want, but whoever cooks with me has to call it gravy or they don't eat.

MAKES 15 CUPS	METHOD
2 pounds boneless pork butt, cut into cubes	1. Coat the meats with the granulated garlic, salt, and pepper.
1 pound split pigs' feet	
¼ pound fatback	2. In a large pot over medium heat add the olive oil. Add the meats and brown everything. Add the onion and garlic and continue until they are golden brown.
1½ tablespoons granulated garlic	
1½ tablespoons kosher salt	
1½ teaspoons freshly ground pepper	3. Lower the heat to low and add the tomatoes. Stir everything in to make sure nothing is sticking to the bottom.
½ cup extra-virgin olive oil	
1 medium yellow onion, diced	4. Cover and let cook for 3 hours or until meat is tender.
¼ cup whole garlic cloves, smashed	
4 28-ounce cans whole San Marzano tomatoes, hand-crushed	5. Stir in a generous amount of basil and the Parmigiano Reggiano. Cook for an additional 10–15 minutes. Remove and discard the pigs' feet.
Fresh basil to taste	
1 tablespoon grated Parmigiano Reggiano	This works well with the meatballs on page 67. Simply pour it over and you have the most amazing Sunday sauce, or alternatively serve over rigatoni with a scoop of ricotta.

Fast Sauce

½ cup extra-virgin olive oil

2 garlic cloves, crushed

1 28-ounce can crushed San Marzano tomatoes

15 cherry tomatoes, cut in half

Kosher salt to taste

Freshly ground pepper to taste

Granulated garlic to taste

Fresh basil to taste

1 tablespoon grated Parmigiano Reggiano

METHOD

1. In a frying pan over medium-high heat, heat up the olive oil. Add the garlic and cook until golden brown.

2. Add the crushed tomatoes and lower the heat to medium. Drop the cherry tomatoes in the sauce. Add the salt, pepper, garlic, basil, and Parmigiano Reggiano. Cook over medium heat for 15 minutes, followed by high heat for 15 minutes, stirring consistently.

3. Season to taste and serve over any pasta. Great for pizzas and sandwiches as well.

Mint Pesto

The classic Pesto Genovese has its origin in the small city of Genova in Liguria, Northern Italy. Here, the Italian gastronomist Giovanni Battista Ratto was the first to officially write down the recipe in 1863. I took this original simple recipe and added mint and a touch of cream, which brings a bit of refreshing sweetness to the recipe. If you would like to keep it traditional, simply do not add the mint.

SERVES 4	METHOD
½ cup pine nuts 3–5 garlic cloves 1½ cups tightly packed fresh basil, plus extra for topping ½ cup tightly packed fresh mint, plus extra for topping ½ cup freshly grated Pecorino Romano, plus extra for topping ½ cup extra-virgin olive oil Kosher salt to taste 1 pound rotini (or your favorite pasta) ½ cup heavy cream	1. Layer the pine nuts in a small skillet over low to medium heat. Toast them for 3–5 minutes, just until brown. Be careful not to burn them, or they'll be no good. Reserve a handful for topping. 2. In a food processor, add the garlic, basil, mint, Pecorino Romano, and pine nuts. Pulse several times until a finely chopped mixture forms. 3. While the food processor is running, begin drizzling in the olive oil until the sauce is fully combined. Add additional olive oil if needed for desired consistency. Taste test for preferred salt level, adding more as needed. 4. Cook your favorite pasta until about half done. Drain the pasta but reserve some of the pasta water. Place the pasta in a frying pan over medium heat, add the pesto, and toss until the pasta is fully covered. Add ¼ cup of the pasta water and the heavy cream, tossing constantly. 5. Taste, salt as needed, and serve. Garnish with a full basil leaf, fresh mint, pine nuts, and Pecorino Romano.

Broccoli Rabe and Sausage over Orecchiette

This dish is great with or without pasta. Mix the broccoli rabe in the frying pan with the sausage, add butter and a bit of chicken broth, and serve.

SERVES 4	METHOD
½ cup extra-virgin olive oil 3 garlic cloves 5 sausages, cut into ½-inch wheels 1 pound orecchiette Broccoli rabe ½ stick unsalted butter Sea salt to taste Juice of 1 lemon ½ cup Parmigiano Reggiano Crushed red pepper flakes to taste	1. In a frying pan over medium heat, heat up the olive oil and garlic. Remove the garlic once golden brown. Drop in the cut sausage and slightly brown them. Cook, adjusting the temperature to make sure you do not burn the oil. 2. Cook the orecchiette until al dente, reserving some of the pasta water. 3. In the frying pan that you cooked the sausage in, add the pasta, broccoli rabe, and butter. Add a ladleful of the pasta water (or chicken broth) and finish cooking the pasta in the frying pan, tossing consistently. Taste and season to taste. Add the lemon juice, Parmigiano Reggiano, and crushed red pepper.

Spaghetti Aglio e Olio

It's amazing what you can do with a handful of ingredients. Spaghetti Aglio e Olio, which translates to "spaghetti with garlic and oil," originated in Southern Italy as a quick and easy meal for poor families. It was made with minimal, readily available, and affordable ingredients, including spaghetti, garlic, olive oil, and chili flakes.

SERVES 4	METHOD
1 pound spaghetti 1 cup olive oil 6 garlic cloves, chopped ½ teaspoon Calabria peppers (Tutto) Parsley, chopped, extra for garnishing Pinch of kosher salt Pinch of freshly ground pepper Juice from 1 large lemon Pecorino Romano	1. Cook the spaghetti al dente, reserving some of the pasta water. 2. Heat the olive oil over medium heat in a large frying pan and toast the garlic. Once the garlic is golden brown, drop in the Calabria peppers, parsley, spaghetti, salt, and pepper. Add a scoop of pasta water, tossing the pasta consistently until the pasta is done. Add the lemon juice. Finish with a generous amount of Pecorino Romano and fresh parsley.

Cacio e Pepe

This is a simple yet complex dish. Do not buy pregrated cheese. It will clump up and make a sticky mess. You must use a fresh brick of cheese.

SERVES 4

1 pound egg taglioni, bucatini, or spaghetti

2 tablespoons unsalted butter, cubed, divided

1 teaspoon freshly cracked black pepper, plus extra for topping

¾ cup finely grated Grana Padano or Parmigiano Reggiano

½ cup finely grated Pecorino Romano, plus extra for topping

METHOD

1. Cook the pasta, stirring occasionally, until al dente, reserving 1 cup of pasta water.

2. Melt 1 tablespoon butter in a Dutch oven or other large pot or skillet over medium heat. Add the pepper and cook, swirling the pan, until toasted, about 1 minute. I prefer to toast the peppercorns, then grind them with a mortar and pestle.

3. Add ½ cup reserved pasta water to the skillet and bring to a simmer. Add the pasta and remaining butter. Reduce heat to low and add the Grana Padano, stirring and tossing with tongs until melted.

4. Remove the pan from the heat and add the Pecorino Romano, stirring and tossing until the cheese melts, the sauce coats the pasta, and the pasta is al dente. (Add more pasta water if the sauce seems dry.) Finish with a bit more pepper and a bit of Pecorino Romano.

Bucatini all'Amatriciana

SERVES 4

1 pound bucatini

½ cup extra-virgin olive oil, plus
more for topping

¼ pound guanciale

½ red onion, chopped

1 6-ounce can tomato paste

¼ teaspoon dry chili flakes or
crushed Calabria peppers (Tutto)

1 14-ounce can crushed San
Marzano tomatoes

10 cherry tomatoes, cut in half

1 cup Pecorino Romano,
plus more for topping

Kosher salt to taste

Freshly ground pepper to taste

METHOD

1. Cook the bucatini, stirring occasionally, until half cooked, reserving 1 cup of pasta water.

2. In a frying pan over high heat, add the olive oil, guanciale, red onion, tomato paste, and chili flakes. Cook down until thick. Add the San Marzano tomatoes and cherry tomatoes. Lower the heat to medium.

3. Remove the bucatini and add to the frying pan with 1 ladle of the pasta water. Add the Pecorino Romano and taste. Add salt and pepper as necessary. Once the pasta is cooked, sprinkle with a bit of olive oil and some Pecorino Romano and serve.

Lemon Pasta with Sesame Seeds and Pecorino Romano

This dish is especially popular in southern Italy and Sicily, regions that are known for their lemon crop. Another example of how good something this easy, made with so few ingredients, can taste.

SERVES 4	METHOD
1 pound linguine 1 teaspoon sesame seeds Pinch of freshly ground pepper 1 stick unsalted butter Zest from 1 lemon, plus extra for garnishing ½ cup Pecorino Romano ½ cup Parmigiano Reggiano Kosher salt to taste	1. Cook the linguine, stirring occasionally, reserving 1 cup of pasta water. 2. Toast the sesame seeds with the pepper and butter in a frying pan. Keep the seeds moving. Toast until brown. 3. Add a ladleful of pasta water to stop the seeds from cooking. Drop the linguine into the frying pan. Add the lemon zest, then the Pecorino Romano and Parmigiano Reggiano. Keep turning until the pasta is done. Salt and pepper to taste. Garnish with lemon zest.

PIZZA DOUGH

CHEESE PIZZA

FRIED CALZONE

BROOKLYN GOURMET CHEESESTEAK

ROLL-N-ROASTER SANDWICH
WITH AU JUS AND CHEESE SAUCE

POTATO/PEPPERS AND EGGS

PIZZA
&
SANDWICHES

Pizza Dough

This is not an exact science, but the
ingredients list will get you a great base.
You might have to adjust as you go.

MAKES 7 SMALL OR 4 LARGE PIZZAS	METHOD
7 cups Caputo 00 flour (available on Amazon) 1½ tablespoons kosher salt 1 tablespoon dry yeast 2 tablespoons extra-virgin olive oil 4 cups water	1. Place the flour, salt, yeast, and olive oil in a mixer on low to medium speed. Gently add the water until a ball is formed, adjusting the flour and water as necessary. 2. Once the dough has formed a ball and is no longer sticking to the sides, remove it from the mixer. 3. Flour a board or countertop and your hands and knead the dough by hand for another minute or so. 4. Let the dough sit for one hour or until it doubles in size. 5. Portion into 7 small balls for a 12-inch pizza or 4 larger balls for a larger pizza. You can freeze the unused dough.

90

Cheese Pizza

MAKES 1 12-INCH PIZZA

Pizza dough (see page 90)

Low-moisture mozzarella (for fresh mozzarella, remove moisture by pressing each piece in a paper towel before adding to the pizza)

4 ounces crushed San Marzano tomatoes

Handful of Pecorino Romano

Handful of Parmigiano Reggiano

Kosher salt to taste

Freshly ground pepper to taste

Extra-virgin olive oil for topping

Fresh basil, hand-torn, for garnishing

METHOD

1. Preheat the oven to 600°F for 45 minutes. Heat is critical to a good pizza.

2. Hand stretch or roll your dough. I like my dough thin, and I build a ¼-inch crust by rolling the edge around.

3. Add either the cheese or the tomatoes first. It's your call. If I have low-moisture mozzarella, I put the cheese down over the dough, then add the tomatoes, Pecorino Romano, Parmigiano Reggiano, salt, and pepper.

4. Bake for about 15 minutes. Finish with olive oil and basil.

Fried Calzone

The Italian translation for *calzone* is "stocking" or "trouser." It is an Italian oven-baked turnover, made with leavened dough, that originated in Naples in the 18th century. A typical calzone is made from salted bread dough, baked in an oven, and stuffed with salami, ham, or vegetables; mozzarella; ricotta; Parmigiano Reggiano or Pecorino Romano; and/or egg. Different regional variations in or on a calzone can often include other ingredients that are normally associated with pizza toppings.

My spin on the traditional baked calzone is to fry the calzone.

MAKES 1 CALZONE	METHOD
Pizza Dough (see page 90)	1. Flatten out a piece of the rested ball of pizza dough with your fingers into a round shape, about 5 inches across. Make it about ⅛-inch thick.
1 cup ricotta	
¼ cup Pecorino Romano	2. Place the appropriate amount of filling on half of the dough and turn over the other half to cover the filling, forming a turnover shape. Do not use so much filling that you have to stretch the dough to cover it. (The stretched dough may break while cooking.) Press the edges firmly with your fingers, then crimp the edges.
½ cup low-moisture mozzarella	
Pinch of kosher salt	
Pinch of freshly ground pepper	
½ teaspoon fresh chopped oregano	3. Lay each calzone on a floured towel or a cookie sheet as the others are completed.
	4. Heat the oil to 350°F in a frying pan large enough to hold 2 calzones at a time. Fry the calzone gently for 5–6 minutes, or until it is a deep golden color, turning it once during cooking. Drain the calzone on a napkin, salt the top, and serve hot. Add pepperoni, spinach, broccolini, leftover Chicken Parmigiana—whatever you want. The great thing about calzones is that you can get creative.

Brooklyn Gourmet Cheesesteak

This will be the best sandwich you have ever made.

SERVES 4

1 small onion, thinly sliced

1 stick unsalted butter

Extra-virgin olive oil

4 garlic cloves

3 yellow peppers, sliced

1 large onion, sliced

Kosher salt to taste

Freshly ground pepper to taste

Garlic powder to taste

8 ounces filet mignon, thinly sliced, and 10 ounces New York strip steak, chopped

Montreal steak seasoning to taste

½ cup heavy cream

1 tablespoon mascarpone

8 slices of provolone, chopped

FOR THE GARLIC BREAD

1 stick salted butter

1 tablespoon dry parsley

5 garlic cloves

Kosher salt to taste

Freshly ground pepper to taste

Large ciabatta loaf

METHOD

1. Place the small onion slices in a saucepan with a stick of butter and cook over low heat until the onions are translucent.

2. Heat up a large frying pan with a generous amount of olive oil over a high heat. Once hot, add the garlic and cook until golden brown. Remove the garlic from the oil and reduce the heat. Add the peppers and large onion slices. Add the salt, pepper, and garlic powder. Remove the peppers and onions when they are about 25% cooked and set aside in a bowl.

3. Preheat the oven to 450°F.

4. To make the garlic bread, blend the butter, parsley, garlic, salt, and pepper in a blender. I prefer to use a hand blender, but if the butter is soft enough, a regular blender will work. Cut the bread in half but do not cut all the way through. Open the bread up and remove some of the inside of the bread. Generously put the garlic spread on both sides of the bread and bake until it's slightly crispy, about 2–3 minutes. Remove from the oven and set aside.

5. Use the same frying pan and add the meat with a bit more olive oil, salt, pepper, and Montréal steak seasoning. Cook for about 1 minute just to get a bit of a sear. Add in the onion sauce, cream, mascarpone, and provolone. Cook over high heat, consistently turning. Once it is all mixed in, add some of the peppers and onions.

6. Load the sandwich with some pepper and onions from the bowl and the meat and cheese mixture. Make sure to add some of the cream sauce to both sides of the bread. Cut and serve.

Roll-N-Roaster Sandwich with Au Jus and Cheese Sauce

A Brooklyn community staple. When in Sheepshead Bay, Brooklyn, a trip to Roll-N-Roaster is a must. The famous sandwich shop uses top-quality roast beef that is slowly roasted, then sliced thinly and piled high onto a freshly baked Kaiser roll, topped off with natural pan gravy and cheese sauce. These sandwiches are the perfect game day sandwich. Serve with french fries.

SERVES 4	METHOD
1 pound Boars Head roast beef 1 16-ounce block Velveeta cheese 4 Kaiser rolls TO MAKE THE AU JUS 2 sticks unsalted butter Pinch of flour ¼ cup red wine 1 cup beef broth, divided Splash of Worcestershire sauce Kosher salt to taste Freshly ground pepper to taste	1. In a saucepan over medium-high heat, melt the butter (or beef drippings), then sprinkle in the flour. Whisk thoroughly until a thin paste forms. 2. Vigorously mix the red wine into the flour mixture. The mixture will likely become purple and gooey. Continue cooking over medium-high heat for 2 minutes or until the sharp alcohol smell is gone. 3. Slowly pour in ½ cup beef broth. Whisk vigorously to combine. Once the beef broth is incorporated, pour in the remaining broth and the Worcestershire sauce. Bring the mixture to a boil and cook for 5 minutes or until slightly thickened and season with salt and pepper. Alternatively, you can buy powdered au jus from the supermarket. 4. Cut a block of Velveeta cheese into ½-inch squares and place in the microwave for 1 minute at a time, stirring after every minute until it is fully melted. If you do not have time to make your own roast beef, have your deli slice up a pound of Boars Head premium roast beef. 5. Slightly toast a Kaiser roll and place it on a large plate (this is messy). Drench both sides of the roll with the au jus. Add ¼ pound of roast beef, more au jus, salt, and pepper. Pour about 1 tablespoon of cheese sauce on the roast beef and put the top of the roll on it. Serve with french fries and the cheese sauce.

Potato/Peppers and Eggs

Many classic Italian recipes came from peasant food. These people made due with what they had and made it taste great because it was made with love and a sense of community. It's always said that Italians cook a lot of food. The family-style way of life was born from feeding entire communities.

There was a time when my family was on public assistance, and we were struggling to make ends meet. The staple was peppers and eggs, and potato and eggs. This is another recipe that takes me back to what most would say was the hardest time in my life, yet it was a time when life was simple. I would not want to go back; however, I am happy and proud to experience these hard times.

SERVES 2	METHOD
½ cup extra-virgin olive oil 2 potatoes, cut into ½-inch cubes Kosher salt to taste 6 to 8 eggs Freshly ground pepper to taste ¼ cup finely chopped fresh parsley ½ cup Parmigiano Reggiano 1 loaf Italian bread 1 stick unsalted butter	1. Heat up a frying pan with olive oil over a medium heat and cook the potatoes until crispy. Salt the potatoes and put aside. Dump the oil out, but leave a bit of a base for the eggs. 2. In a separate bowl, combine the eggs, salt, pepper, parsley, and Parmigiano Reggiano. Beat the eggs and pour them into the frying pan that you cooked the potatoes in. Drop the potatoes into the egg mixture and cook. You can try to flip it like a frittata, but I prefer to scramble it. 3. Preheat the oven to 350°F. 4. Cut a loaf of Italian bread in half lengthwise. Bake in the oven until crispy, about 2–3 minutes. Butter the bread, add the salt and pepper, and load the sandwich with the eggs. This can be served on a plate as well. For peppers and eggs, substitute the potatoes for 1 yellow pepper and 1 red pepper.

MAC AND CHEESE

WATERMELON ARUGULA SALAD

BROCCOLI RABE

GARLIC BREAD

TOMATO AND AVOCADO SALAD

SICILIAN POTATOES

LUKE'S ROASTED PUMPKIN SEEDS

ZUCCHINE CON NOCCIOLE E RICOTTA

SIDES

Mac and Cheese

SERVES 6

1 pound ziti or elbows

2 ounces provolone

4½ ounces white cheddar

1 stick unsalted butter

1½ cups heavy cream

Kosher salt to taste if needed

10–15 slices of American cheese

METHOD

1. Cook the ziti, stirring occasionally, reserving 1 cup of pasta water. Run the ziti under cold water to stop the cooking process and set aside.

2. Chop up the provolone and cheddar cheeses and add to a large frying pan with butter and heavy cream over medium heat, stirring constantly until everything is melted. Do not burn the cheese or you must start over.

3. Add the ziti to the mixture and stir. Taste and adjust salt if necessary. (Depending on how much salt you use in the pasta water, you might need to add salt, but the cheese usually is salty enough to carry the dish.)

4. Serve as is or place the mixture in a lasagna pan, top with American cheese, and bake at 375°F for approximately 30 minutes until the cheese is bubbling.

Watermelon Arugula Salad

This is a wonderful summer salad. I prefer dried bitter black olives, but you can use whatever you want. My wife hates olives, so I leave them out when I am making this for her.

SERVES 6

12 ounces arugula

Seedless watermelon, diced in 1-inch cubes

½ cup black pitted olives

⅛ teaspoon fresh mint, chopped fine (add more to taste)

⅓ cup crumbled feta

¼ cup Parmigiano Reggiano, shaved

FOR THE DRESSING

2 tablespoons champagne or white wine vinegar

Pinch of kosher salt

Pinch of freshly ground pepper

6 tablespoons extra-virgin olive oil

METHOD

Mix the arugula, watermelon, olives, mint, and dressing. Serve and garnish with the feta and Parmigiano Reggiano.

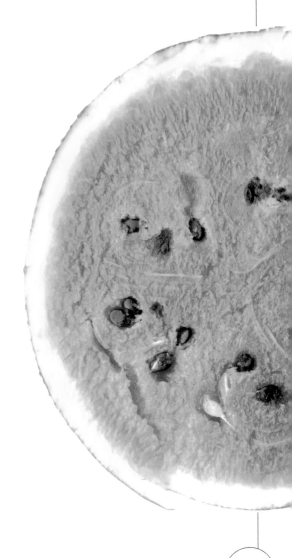

Broccoli Rabe

SERVES 4

1 cup extra-virgin olive oil

4 garlic cloves

1 bunch broccoli rabe (remove the woody stems)

½ cup chicken stock

¼ teaspoon crushed red pepper flakes

Kosher salt to taste

METHOD

Heat a saucepan with olive oil over a medium heat and cook the garlic until golden brown. Place the broccoli rabe in the pan with the chicken stock, red pepper flakes, and salt. Cook until the broccoli rabe is fork-tender.

Garlic Bread

SERVES 4

4 garlic cloves

2 sticks unsalted butter

¼ cup chopped parsley

Kosher salt to taste

Freshly ground pepper to taste

1 loaf of ciabatta

Parmigiano Reggiano (optional)

1. Preheat the oven to 350°F.

2. Mix the first five ingredients in a blender. Season to taste. Spread on ciabatta bread and bake until crispy, about 2–3 minutes. If you'd like, sprinkle Parmigiano Reggiano before baking.

Tomato and Avocado Salad

SERVES 4

24 ounces cherry tomatoes,
cut in half

2 avocados, cut into ⅓-inch cubes

1 small red onion (or half of a
medium red onion), thinly sliced

4 tablespoons chopped cilantro

Juice of 2 lemons

Extra-virgin olive oil

Kosher salt to taste

Freshly ground pepper to taste

METHOD

1. In a large bowl, combine the tomatoes, avocados, red onions, and cilantro.

2. In a separate bowl, whisk together the lemon juice, olive oil, salt, and pepper.

3. Pour the dressing over the tomato, avocado, red onion, and cilantro and mix in. Adjust with salt, pepper, olive oil, and lemon as needed.

Sicilian Potatoes

SERVES 4	METHOD
2 pounds baby Yukon gold potatoes, quartered ¼ cup olive oil 4 garlic cloves, chopped Sea salt and freshly ground pepper to taste 3 sprigs fresh rosemary, chopped 2 cups Pecorino Romano 1 stick unsalted butter, sliced	1. Preheat the oven to 400°F. 2. Put the potatoes in a bowl, add the olive oil, garlic, sea salt and pepper, rosemary, and Pecorino Romano, and mix thoroughly with your hands. Put the mixture in a roasting pan and add the butter slices over the top. Bake for about 45 minutes, turning the potatoes when they begin to brown (after about 15 minutes). Taste and adjust seasonings as desired.

Luke's Roasted Pumpkin Seeds

The perfect post-Halloween snack.

MAKES 2 CUPS	METHOD
2 cups pumpkin seeds 1 tablespoon olive oil Kosher salt 1 tablespoon brown sugar ½ teaspoon cinnamon	1. Preheat the oven to 400°F. 2. Toss the pumpkin seeds in the olive oil, salt, brown sugar, and cinnamon. 3. Lightly coat a sheet pan with olive oil and evenly distribute the pumpkin seeds. 4. Bake for 15 minutes or until both sides are golden brown. Let cool and serve.

Zucchine con Nocciole e Ricotta

SERVES 4

3 medium summer squash or zucchini (or pattypan squash!), cut in half lengthwise

1½ teaspoons kosher salt, plus more to taste

¼ cup blanched hazelnuts

6 tablespoons extra-virgin olive oil, divided, plus more for drizzling

1 small bunch mint, divided

1 small garlic clove, finely grated

2 tablespoons white wine vinegar

¾ teaspoon sugar

½ teaspoon crushed red pepper flakes

Freshly ground pepper to taste

½ large lemon

½ cup fresh ricotta

Sea salt

Toasted Italian bread

METHOD

1. Preheat the oven to 300°F.

2. Toss the squash and salt in a colander and set over a bowl. Let sit for 10 minutes, then pat dry with paper towels.

3. Toss the hazelnuts and 1 tablespoon oil on a rimmed baking sheet and roast, shaking occasionally, until golden brown, 15–20 minutes. Let cool, then crush into large pieces with a measuring cup or glass.

4. Chop 3 mint sprigs and mix in a large bowl with the garlic, vinegar, sugar, red pepper flakes, and 2 tablespoons oil; set aside.

5. Heat 3 tablespoons oil in a large skillet over medium-high heat, add the squash, and cook for about 5 minutes. Reduce heat to medium-low and cover. Continue to cook until the squash is very tender, about 15 minutes. Transfer to a cutting board.

6. Cut the squash into 2-inch pieces and toss in the dressing; season with salt and pepper. Let sit at room temperature.

7. Zest the lemon half into a small bowl, mix in the ricotta and remaining tablespoon of olive oil, and season with sea salt.

8. Spread the lemon ricotta over the platter. Top with the squash and their juices. Squeeze the lemon over. Finish with the remaining mint, the hazelnuts, olive oil, and salt.

9. Toast and cut a loaf of Italian bread.

FIREBALL FRENCH TOAST

LEMON RICOTTA PANCAKES

FIG TOAST

THE HANGOVER BREAKFAST SANDWICH

BREAKFAST

Fireball French Toast

The perfect morning comfort food (not for kids). This recipe was created while on a ski trip with five families. My great friend Nick was handing out mini Fireball bottles to stuff in our pockets for the slopes. Since I wound up taking over breakfast, I decided to do something different. Since then it has become a winter favorite.

SERVES 6

FOR THE FIREBALL FLAMBE
½ stick unsalted butter
Splash of apple or orange juice
¼ cup blueberries
¼ cup sliced strawberries
¼ cup sliced bananas
1 tablespoon brown sugar
Fireball
Kosher salt to taste

FOR THE FRENCH TOAST
2 eggs
½ teaspoon vanilla extract (natural)
¼ cup brown sugar
1 teaspoon cinnamon
Dash of nutmeg
1 cup milk
Loaf of soft bread such as brioche, or 6 croissants
2 sticks unsalted butter

METHOD

1. Cook the butter, apple or orange juice, blueberries, strawberries, and bananas over low heat. After they warm up, add the brown sugar. Once the fruit is softened a bit, add a few shots of Fireball and let it cook out. If it is becoming too thick, add a bit of water. Add a dash of salt and taste to adjust as necessary.

2. Mix the eggs, vanilla, brown sugar, cinnamon, and nutmeg in a bowl. Be sure to beat it thoroughly. Add the milk and continue to mix in. Cut the bread into thick slices and soak in the egg batter. In a frying pan over medium heat, melt the butter. Once the butter is melted, put the bread in the pan and brown both sides. Sprinkle some cinnamon and brown sugar as you turn.

3. Plate the bread and pour the Fireball Flambé over it. Serve immediately to preserve the crunch of the bread.

Lemon Ricotta Pancakes

Everything about these sweet and zesty pancakes is delightful. Finish with maple syrup, a flambé, or refer to my Fireball French Toast recipe to finish. This is a quick-and-easy impressive breakfast that everyone loves. Simply grab your favorite pancake batter. I prefer Stonewall Kitchen buttermilk pancake and waffle mix.

SERVES 1	METHOD
¼ cup ricotta 1 cup completely mixed batter Zest of 1 lemon Pinch of kosher salt 2 tablespoons lemon marmalade Capful of Orzata almond syrup or almond extract Unsalted butter Maple syrup	1. Mix the ricotta into the pancake batter. 2. Add the lemon zest and salt. Place the marmalade in a coffee cup and heat in the microwave for about 15 seconds to soften, then add to the batter and mix thoroughly with an electric hand mixer. Taste and add more lemon marmalade if necessary. The lemon taste should be a hint, not overwhelming. 3. Add the Orzata almond syrup. 4. Cook over low heat in a heavily buttered frying pan or skillet until golden brown on each side. 5. Serve with a dab of butter and side of maple syrup. Alternatively, use the Fireball Flambé from my French toast recipe (see page 116).

Fig Toast

While traveling in Capri, I stumbled upon a Neapolitan breakfast that was light, refreshing, and delicious. They used yogurt as the base, but I had to change it up to create the best fast and healthy breakfast or snack.

SERVES 1

1 teaspoon mascarpone

½ cup ricotta (whipped)

Zest of ¼ lemon

Pinch of sea salt

1 1-inch piece toasted Italian bread
(I prefer ciabatta)

5 fresh fig halves

1 tablespoon sunflower seeds

Honey for garnishing

Fresh mint for garnishing

METHOD

1. Whisk the mascarpone and ricotta with the lemon zest and salt. Do not use too much salt or lemon zest; we are looking for a hint of flavor.

2. Toast a slice of your favorite Italian bread. Spread the mixture on top of the bread and finish with the fig halves, sunflower seeds, honey, and a mint leaf.

The Hangover Breakfast Sandwich

SERVES 1

1 English muffin, bagel, or any other bread, cut in half

2 slices of American cheese

2 slices of bacon

2 large eggs

Unsalted butter

Kosher salt to taste

Freshly ground pepper to taste

METHOD

1. Grill both sides of the English muffin, bagel, or bread.

2. Place a slice of American cheese on the hot side of each slice and set aside.

3. Put 2 tablespoons water in a frying pan and cook 2 slices of bacon. The water will crisp out the bacon. Remove at desired texture and put on both halves of the English muffin, bagel, or toast. Dump the remaining grease from the pan and wipe it out with a paper towel.

4. Cook the eggs overeasy; we want the yolk to break in the sandwich. Add the salt and pepper and assemble your sandwich. Serve with Advil, coffee, and a lot of napkins.

INDEX